Pretty Red Wing

The riverboat *Quincy* at
Red Wing, August 18, 1896.

Pretty Red Wing
Historic
River Town

Patricia Condon Johnston

For Mrs. Oliver R. Wilson
I'm glad we met.
Enjoy
Patricia Condon Johnston

Johnston Publishing Inc.
Afton, Minnesota

Cover: This illustration appeared on the sheet
music for "Red Wing," written by Kerry Mills and
published by F. A. Mills in New York in 1907.

Also by Patricia Condon Johnston
Stillwater: Minnesota's Birthplace
Eastman Johnson's Lake Superior Indians
Minnesota's Irish

Address inquiries to:
Johnston Publishing Inc.
Box 96
Afton, MN 55001

Library of Congress Catalog Card Number 83-080138
ISBN 0-942934-27-X

for my grandmother,
Mary Hortense Gallagher Braaten

Red Wing residents turned out en masse for this turn-of-the-century parade on Main Street. The building on the extreme right is the Music Hall, built in 1867. The advertisement for books was displayed by a bookstore at the present location of the Koehler Book and Stationery Store.

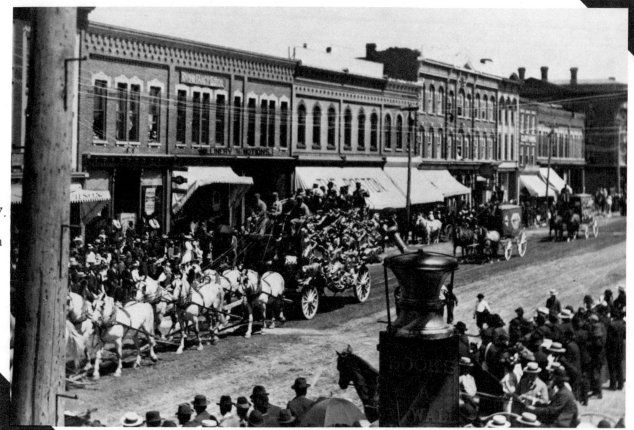

Contents

Preface

Preservation is the word of the hour in Red Wing. Putting her best foot forward, the town is in the midst of a well-planned revival to refurbish her Victorian image. This is exactly as it should be. From her earliest years, pretty Red Wing has placed importance on her past. Her first settler, missionary Joseph Hancock, wrote the first history of Goodhue County. Only a few years ago, during the Bicentennial year, Madeline Angell Johnson of Red Wing compiled a remarkably comprehensive history of the city that relied both on the efforts of earlier historians as well as research assembled by numerous local residents.

Much of the credit for the current renewal belongs to these and like-minded residents who point with pride to Red Wing's accomplishments. This is no ordinary city. Rather, she has been nurtured by several generations of able and generous men and women with an eye to her best interests. Trading Indian garb for Victorian finery, pretty Red Wing came of age as a wheat queen and world-famous pottery maker; her youthful prosperity is flaunted in her downtown and residential architecture. What matters now is keeping up appearances. The present is upon her, but pretty Red Wing is no less a nineteenth-century river town at heart.

This book is my personal tribute to pretty Red Wing. It began as a magazine article that appeared in *Twin Cities* magazine in 1981. At that time and in the three years since, many people have helped me with this project. In Red Wing, these include Jean Chesley and the staff at the Goodhue County Historical Museum: Orville Olson, Beatrice Gronvall, and Ethel Dunn; Mayor Ed Powderly; Anna Lisa Tooker at the Red Wing Public Library; Dennis Welsch, Red Wing's planning coordinator; and Carrie Conklin, the city's preservation planner.

10

I am also grateful to my former editor at *Twin Cities* magazine, John
Hodowanic, who assigned the original article and prepared it for publication.
Ken Carley, another editor with whom I have worked, supplied the sheet
music for the cover of *Pretty Red Wing* from his personal collection. Ken was
the editor of *Minnesota History*, published by the Minnesota Historical
Society, for thirteen years, from 1968 until 1980. Except for the photograph of
Frances Densmore, which is from the National Anthropological Archives at
the Smithsonian Institution, most of the historic photographs in this book are
owned by the Goodhue County Historical Museum in Red Wing.

Dale Johnston designed *Pretty Red Wing* and saw it through production. To
my mind it is an exceptionally beautiful book and one that speaks for his
enormous talent. Dale also designed three earlier books produced by Johnston
Publishing, *Stillwater: Minnesota's Birthplace, Eastman Johnson's Lake
Superior Indians* and *Minnesota's Irish*. Rohland Wiltfang has been
production consultant for all four books.

Especially, I am indebted to my husband, Charlie, who made it possible for me
to write this book. Being the extraordinary man that he is, he also helped with
it in other ways. Some of the photographs included in *Pretty Red Wing* are
his. He likewise assisted with the research, read manuscript, and proofread
galleys. I really appreciate your contribution to this book, Charlie.
It is what it is in large part because of you.

This view of Red Wing
dates to about 1890. The
domed courthouse,
slightly to the right of
center, was built on the
site of the current
courthouse in 1859 and
demolished in 1931.

The Red Wing Dynasty

Pretty Red Wing was born an Indian princess. Her Dakota people called her Remnicha, meaning wood, hills, and water. They lived in bark lodges and skin-covered cone-shaped tepees at the river's edge. Higher up, around the base of Barn Bluff, they tended fields of corn and squash. One after another, for several generations, the chiefs at this Indian village were known as Red Wing.

The name connoted a dynasty. Whoo-pa-doo-ta or Hoo-pa-hoo-sha (Wing of Scarlet) was Chief Red Wing in the mid-1700s. The French called him L'Aile Rouge (Red Wing) because he carried a swan's wing dyed scarlet as his talisman. Spoken of as a bold and dynamic leader, Whoo-pa-doo-ta took part in Pontiac's Conspiracy against the British at the end of the French and Indian War. Except that he had a hand in that conflict, this Chief Red Wing might have escaped the notice of historians altogether. As it is, other than these few scraps of commentary, nothing more has been recorded about him.

Red Wing's son, Tatankamani (Walking Buffalo), also called Red Wing, was chief at the Dakota encampment at the head of Lake Pepin when Lieutenant Zebulon Pike came upriver in 1805 to negotiate a site for Fort Snelling. Pike mentions him in his diary: "He made me a speech and presented a pipe, pouch, and buffalo skin. He appeared to be a man of good sense, and promised to accompany me to St. Peters [the Minnesota River]; he saluted me, and had it returned. I made him a small present." This gift may have been the silver Jefferson peace medal dated 1801 that was found on a skeleton, believed to be Tatankamani, during a street grading project in Red Wing in 1871. The medal was afterwards acquired by the Minnesota Historical Society.

Tatankamani's name is listed on the treaty Pike concluded with the Indians, but the chief did not sign it. Pike also tried to impress the idea of American sovereignty upon the Minnesota Dakota. Nonetheless, Tatankamani was probably among those Indians who sided with the British against the Americans during the War of 1812. Once the hostilities ended, he was one of several Dakota chiefs who signed treaties of peace and friendship with the

United States government. In 1827 Lawrence Taliaferro, the Indian agent at Fort Snelling, called Tatankamani a "firm and unshaken friend of the Americans."

Following Tatankamani's death in 1829, he was succeeded by Wacouta (The Shooter). For reasons that seem rooted in heredity, this third Chief Red Wing was initially rejected by some of his tribe. Perhaps Wacouta was part white. One source states that Tatankamani married an English trader's daughter; this would make Wacouta a mixed-blood. It is also possible that Wacouta was Tatankamani's nephew or stepson. In any case, the Indians sought Lawrence Taliaferro's advice as to who should be chief. When the agent refused to be a party to the decision, insisting that the Indians settle the matter among themselves, they chose Wacouta.

According to a pioneer missionary who met Wacouta in 1849, the chief was "very tall, straight and dignified in his demeanor. He was…a man of good judgement. His authority was not absolute. He rather advised his people than commanded them. He encouraged industry and sobriety." A second early missionary added that while Wacouta was generally mild-mannered, he was "very decided" in his opinions. "Opposition only stirred him to act with more firmness and determination," he said. "He was, on the whole, such a man as one would much rather have for a friend than an enemy."

Wacouta welcomed white settlers to his valley. The notion of civilization appealed to him. In 1837 he had been one of twenty-six Dakota chiefs and warriors who accompanied Lawrence Taliaferro to Washington. The Indians were entertained at the Globe Hotel for three weeks and presented with medals. Some of them had their portraits painted. But if the tribesmen were overwhelmed at such largess, they were predictably duped by their hosts. The United States government wanted Dakota lands and they got them. The treaty specified substantial annuities in the form of goods and money spread over a twenty-year period; the Indians signed away their homelands east of the Mississippi. Wacouta's village site was not immediately affected by the transaction, but he would lose it soon enough.

Noted archeologist T. H. Lewis identified several hundred Indian mounds in the Red Wing area in the 1880s. A number of these were effigy mounds shaped like snakes.

An Indian Swan Song

The first missionaries to reach Wacouta's village were two Calvinists from Switzerland, Samuel Denton and Daniel Gavin. Sponsored by the Evangelical Missionary Society of Lausanne, they established the only Protestant mission of its kind in the Northwest at Red Wing.

Samuel Denton arrived in Red Wing in 1837 accompanied by his new wife, formerly Persis Skinner, who had been a teacher at the mission school at Mackinac. He was joined the next year by Daniel Gavin who soon afterwards married Lucy Stevens, a teacher at the Lake Harriet mission in what is now Minneapolis. The two log mission buildings this group erected were located

It has been suggested that the architect who designed the administration building at the Minnesota State Training School, built in 1891 in Red Wing, patterned it after castles found along the Rhine. This photograph of a boys' drill at the school was taken early in this century.

near the northeast corner of Bush and Third streets. They were substantial houses, clapboarded on the outside and boarded on the interior, where the families lived and conducted classes for the Indians. Fenced vegetable gardens surrounded the houses.

A few of the Indians were taught to read and write, and many of them learned farming and gardening. In July, 1838, Persis Denton sent a note to General Henry Sibley in St. Paul thanking him for sending seeds to the mission. "Could you see how finely they are growing in our beautiful garden, I am sure you would be glad with us," she told him. For his part, Wacouta made inquiries into the Christian religion, asking the missionaries to teach him to say morning and evening prayers. If there were new roads to be walked, perhaps he would break trail. He wished to try to serve God, he said. Even so, the mission was never much of a success.

As year after hard year wore on, the Indians became increasingly unfriendly toward the missionaries and suspicious of their motives. The mission families also quarreled among themselves. By 1845, when both families abandoned the mission, Lucy Gavin's health had been broken, and Samuel Denton was suffering with a heart ailment. While it is doubtful that these first missionaries made any conversions, an Indian named Ehnamani (Walks Amongst), born in the Red Wing village in 1825, was one of their pupils. Ehnamani later trained for the ministry and served as pastor of the large Dakota Pilgrim Congregational Church at Santee, Nebraska.

In 1848, taking up the work begun by the Swiss missionaries, the American Board for Foreign Missions assigned two Presbyterian ministers, Joseph Hancock and John Aiton, to Red Wing. Hancock had been born in the East, in New Hampshire, and Aiton was from Scotland. Each man brought a wife and baby daughter to the Indian country. Since one of the mission houses was being occupied by John Bush and his family (Bush had been hired by the government to teach the Indians to farm), the Hancocks and the Aitons shared a single one-story dwelling with a loft where they also taught school in half of the downstairs.

When Minnesota became a territory in 1849, Red Wing was home to 306 Indians: 95 men, 99 women, and 112 children. Except for the mission buildings, the village consisted solely of nineteen bark lodges belonging to the Dakota. These pole-framed structures, covered with bark, stood along the river close to where Main Street is now, between Bush and Potter streets. Artist Henry Lewis came upriver from St. Louis and painted his well-known landscape of the picturesque community about this time. Seth Eastman, a career officer stationed at Fort Snelling in the 1840s, also made a pencil drawing of Red Wing's village. These are her earliest known portraits.

Prairie Island Indians, parading on Third Street during a street fair about 1900, recall the town's Indian origins.

Joseph Hancock, Red Wing's first permanent settler, was born on April 4, 1816, in Orford, New Hampshire. He trained for the ministry at the Mission Institute in Quincy, Illinois, where his courses included Hebrew, Greek, and Latin. A modest and devout man, he lived the life he preached to others.

In a letter dated 1849 to the secretary of the American Board in Boston, John Aiton praised Red Wing's natural charms: her luxuriant vegetation, rich black soil, and fresh water springs. Given her favorable position on the west bank of the Father of Rivers, he thought it likely that the place would one day be a county seat—"when the White man plows the Red man's grave." Even so, Aiton quickly lost interest in the Red Wing mission. First of all, there was some unpleasant business with the American Board concerning his salary. He also differed with Hancock as to how the school should be run. As a result, in 1850 he packed up and moved his family from Red Wing, leaving Hancock to carry on the mission work singlehandedly.

Joseph Hancock was Red Wing's first permanent white settler. He also ranks as her patron saint. Ministering at the start to the Indians, then to incoming whites, he gained the respect and admiration of both races and served in civil as well as religious capacities.

In the beginning, when the Indians were his primary concern, the missionary set about trying to convert them by first learning their language. This effort was not lost on the Dakota who liked Hancock and responded to his interest. At nine and again at one o'clock, he called the children to classes with a large hand bell which he had purchased in St. Paul. At dismissal time the pupils were rewarded with raisins and crackers. Within a year of his arrival, he was able to report to his home office that "all read and spell from the blackboard in their own language. The more advanced also *write* on slates."

The frontier took its toll in his personal life, however. Less than two years after coming to Red Wing, his wife, Maria, died following the birth of the couple's second child and first son, Willie. When he was thirteen months old, little Willie followed his mother to the grave. Both were buried near the mission house, but their remains were later moved to Oakwood Cemetery. Because he asked them to, the Aitons returned briefly to Red Wing to help the bereaved missionary. After they left, Hancock sent his three-year-old daughter, Marilla, to live temporarily with a missionary family in St. Paul.

In 1851 Territorial Governor Alexander Ramsey appointed Joseph Hancock Red Wing's first postmaster. He was likewise Goodhue County's first register of deeds and first superintendent of schools. The Presbyterian Church he built in 1857 was Red Wing's first church building. (Hancock personally collected donations for this building, supplementing this sum with a settlement he had recently received from a railroad for injuries sustained in an accident.) Added to this list of firsts, Joseph Hancock wrote the first history of Goodhue County. He also served as the first president of two organizations: the Old Settlers Association and the Red Wing Historical Society.

At the time of his death at the age of ninety-one in 1907, Joseph Hancock was Red Wing's most highly esteemed citizen. Two years earlier, townspeople had filled the rooms of the new Carnegie-Lawther Library for the presentation of a lifesize bronze bust of the missionary, the gift of Mrs. E. W. Brooks. Edmund Brooks, addressing the group for his mother, called Hancock "a man who always stood for that which is highest and best in American citizenship, a patriot and educator, a Christian gentleman." During more than a half century in Red Wing, Joseph Hancock had outlived three wives. (He is buried with all three at Oakwood Cemetery.) He had also witnessed enormous change in his chosen land. Red Wing had become a bustling city of ten thousand people.

White settlement in Red Wing followed treaties signed with the Minnesota Dakota in 1851. Like most of the Indians, Wacouta and his band had opposed the sale of their lands. "The graves of their kindred dead were here," wrote Joseph Hancock. "This had been for many years their hunting ground. The majority of them were born here. It was natural they should desire to remain here." But the Indians were given little choice. Officiating government commissioners alternately bullied and cajoled, ridiculed and threatened the Indians. "Suppose your Great Father wanted your lands and did not want a treaty for your good, he could come with a hundred thousand men and drive you off to the Rocky Mountains," the tribesmen were told. In exchange for pennies an acre and a narrow ribbon of a reservation along the upper Minnesota River, the Indians relinquished what amounted to the southern two-thirds of Minnesota.

Joseph Hancock's grave, second from left, is flanked by those of his three wives and two of his children at Oakwood Cemetery.

Charles Johnston

Even before Congress ratified the ill-gotten agreements, white settlers began marking off their 160-acre claims in Red Wing and putting up shanties. Early in 1853 the Indians were routed once and for all from the new townsite when an unknown incendiary set fire to their lodges. In less than a half hour, while the population looked on dumbfounded, the Dakota village lay in ashes. That same year Goodhue County was created. (It is named for James Madison Goodhue, a New England-born journalist who published Minnesota's first newspaper, the *Minnesota Pioneer*, in St. Paul in 1849.) Red Wing was chosen county seat.

Ridding Red Wing of its Indians was not quite that simple, however. For the next several years, though resentment against them was mounting, they were often seen about town. This was before the Dakota War of 1862. In the aftermath of that bloody outbreak, the Indians forfeited their reservation lands and were ousted from the state. Virtually all of the Minnesota Dakota were herded aboard overcrowded boats and shipped downriver. In St. Louis they were transferred to an even more overcrowded steamer and sent up the Missouri River to Crow Creek (in what is now southeastern South Dakota). Wacouta was among the many Indians who perished at this desolate place for lack of provisions. He was about seventy years old. After three years at Crow Creek, the survivors were moved to Santee, Nebraska, where the government conducted a manual labor school and religious groups operated two boarding schools. Many of the Dakota spent the remaining years of their lives at Santee, but not all of them were content to do so. By the 1880s, with little government interference, Red Wing Indians were filtering back to their homeland.

Most of them settled at Prairie Island (within Red Wing's present city limits) where poor farmland was attracting few whites. In 1890 the Goodhue County census listed sixty Indians at Prairie Island. They were living in abject poverty and were a constant drain on the Goodhue County poor fund. Early in 1895 the *Hastings Democrat* reported the death of an Indian woman from starvation on Prairie Island, observing that all of the Indians in the locality were in want of the necessities of life. Urging its readers to be charitable, the paper pointed out that the Indians "cannot make their wants known, and they don't know how to work, and could not obtain employment if they did." The county was willing enough to bury Indians at public expense but had no funds to provide medical care for them.

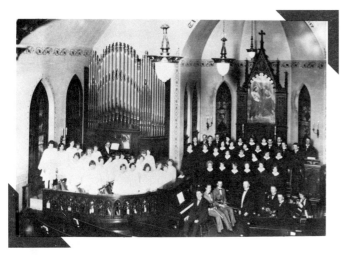

The girls' choir, adult choir, and accompanying musicians at Trinity Lutheran Church (now United Lutheran) about 1928.

Ironically, a nuclear power plant built in the 1970s, Red Wing's main source of revenue, now shares Prairie Island with the Indians. Their community numbers about 125 persons. Some of the men work seasonally for neighboring farmers and as construction and factory workers in Red Wing. Public assistance continues to be an important source of support for the Indians, but this may not be the case for much longer. The reason is that Prairie Island Bingo came to Red Wing in 1984. If the game lives up to the expectations of its promoters, Prairie Island Indians may finally enjoy some measure of affluence.

In downtown Red Wing, the former site of Chief Wacouta's lodge at the corner of Main and Plum streets is marked by a historical plaque. The last Chief Red Wing was Hazen Wakute, Wacouta's grandson, who was born at Santee in 1884. He was educated on the reservation and attended Flandreau High School in Flandreau, South Dakota, and the Pipestone Indian School at Pipestone, Minnesota. During World War I he enlisted in the army and served as a saddler in the third company of the 164th Depot Brigade. In later years he was a familiar and popular figure in Red Wing, something of a city mascot, who enjoyed appearing in parades both in Red Wing and elsewhere. Chief Hazen Wakute died at the Veterans Hospital in Minneapolis in 1949; he was buried with military honors at Fort Snelling National Cemetery.

Left to right: the Charles
Betcher Millwork Com-
pany, the Charles Betcher
Sawmill Company, and
the Levee Street City
Water Pumping Station.
This is where the lower
harbor is today.

Pioneer Beginnings

Putting her Indian past behind her, pretty Red Wing came into her own as a beguiling Victorian. Her pioneers were a hardy and diversified lot that included farmers and tradesmen, doctors and hotel keepers, all with high hopes of making their fortunes in the newly-acquired territory. Most were Americans, born in the East, but there was also an influx of Scandinavians and Germans. In 1853 the village was surveyed and platted for its proprietors: William Freeborn, Benjamin Hoyt, Charles Willis, and Alexander Ramsey.

John Hancock quoted a Swedish immigrant concerning an irregularity connected with land claims in 1853: "As the new settlers could not carry surveying instruments, it was customary to pace out the lines and distances, which almost invariably resulted in large quarter sections. I was somewhat surprised to find by the government survey the next year, the claim I had paced off for my quarter section, held land enough for about two more." The settler also observed that "our American friends selected those who were capable of taking long strides to do their measuring."

Hotels were needed to accommodate the rush of new arrivals and the first to go up was the Red Wing House on the corner of Main and Bush streets. Its owner was Andrus Durand who hired it built by carpenters Hiram and Joseph Middaugh during the winter of 1852-53. The lumber was rafted downstream from Stillwater. It was later renamed the Tee-Pee-Tonka (Big House).

Several more hotels including the American House, the Elder House, and the National House were open for business by 1857, but travelers could still have trouble finding a place to sleep. Mrs. Joseph Ullmann, the wife of a pioneer St. Paul merchant, returning from a spring buying trip to Chicago and St. Louis with her husband that year, recalled being stranded in Red Wing during a fierce rain storm:

"The landlord of the Red Wing Hotel was not glad to see six dripping figures coming into his house already filled with guests. With reluctance he allowed us two women to enter the 'parlor'; but, when my husband came to ask if we wished anything, he gruffly said, 'Cant go in there: Gents aint allowed.' We could remain, the landlord said, if we would accept the accommodations he would give us. This was a bed in a large room in the upper story where sleeping places could be arranged for forty or fifty persons, or a bunk in the hallway."

Goodhue County's medical history begins with the arrival of Dr. William W. Sweney in Red Wing in 1852. Born in Pennsylvania, Sweney was a graduate of the Rush Medical College of Chicago. In 1853 it was Dr. Sweney who cared for seventeen cholera victims who reached Red Wing by steamboat. After isolating them in a makeshift hospital, he not only nursed ten of them back to health, but also managed to keep the disease from spreading. Later in his career Dr. Sweney was elected president of the Minnesota State Medical Association in 1873.

Dr. Sweney was also an avid outdoorsman who enjoyed nothing so much as trout fishing. Among the first items of information he obtained from the Indians, he said, was that the small spring brooks teemed with the fish. Better still, the Indians considered them taboo and never ate them. To do so would be to anger the gods and invite disease, they believed. In an hour or two spent on a stream in the evening, the good doctor could net eight or ten pounds of the speckled beauties. Once, having befriended Wacouta, he invited the chief to share a trout supper with him:

"[Wacouta] consented to be present, provided we would lock the doors, eat dinner upstairs, hang a curtain before the windows, and say nothing of what he had eaten. This was done, and old 'Shooter' made a very hearty meal...but I thought, during the trout course, that he acted as though the morsels were hard to swallow, like a boy bolting his first oyster, and that qualms of conscience interfered with deglutitation. He ate frequently with me afterwards, but I cannot say that trout ever appeared to be a favorite dish with him."

The Blatz Milwaukee Beer Depot was located near the La Grange flour mill. (This later became the Bay State Milling Company and burned in 1945.) The man in the white shirt is Al Rehder. This picture was taken about 1910.

In the fall of 1852, Dr. Sweney organized a commercial fishing enterprise with a few friends. Their fishing grounds were about a mile above Bay City on the Wisconsin side of the Mississippi River. Within a short time the men were able to supply St. Paul with forty barrels of salted fish at six dollars a barrel. They took only the best fish for their purposes, said Sweney, rejecting pike, pickerel, bass, sturgeon, dogfish, sheephead, and gars. What they wanted were "rich, fat and luscious cat, buffalo, and carp." While some might scoff at this selection, Dr. Sweney explained that they only wanted such fish as would repay them in nourishment during the coming winter. "Pike, pickerel, bass and trout, as salted fish," he said, "are about as nutrient as floating islands…and all are measurably worthless as food to strong, hearty working men."

This street scene at Bush and Third streets dates to the 1880s. Dr. O. J. Brown was one of several physicians who came to Red Wing during that decade.

The date is May 18, 1899. These businessmen are repairing Webster's Way, the path to the summit of Barn Bluff, built by earlier volunteers in 1889 under the direction of C. C. Webster. Boulders needed to be removed each spring and the earthen steps reconstructed. A picnic always followed.

In 1929 Webster's Way was replaced by the Citizens Memorial Stairway, consisting of 472 concrete steps. Each step was sold for ten dollars and carried the name of its donor. More than a hundred of these steps are still in place near the top of the west end of the bluff. Others were ripped out during the construction of the Eisenhower Bridge in 1958 and consigned to a city gravel pit. In 1975 those steps that had been scrapped, but were still usable, were reinstalled at the east end of Barn Bluff.

Dr. Sweney was also an amateur archeologist who made extensive studies of the Indian mounds in and around Red Wing. Although little evidence of them now remains, there were numerous Indian earthworks in the vicinity, including about fifty mounds within the present city. Fort Swency, near Welch, Minnesota, is named for Dr. Sweney and his son, Dr. William M. Sweney, who later practiced medicine with his father and shared his interest in archeology. Some of the many Indian artifacts the Sweneys uncovered are at the Goodhue County Historical Museum in Red Wing.

While several of Red Wing's pioneer homes were log cabins with dirt floors, William Freeborn (whose sister Maria was married to Dr. Sweney) built the first frame house in town for his family in the spring of 1853. It was two stories high with piped-in water supplied by a hydraulic pump placed in a nearby pond. Freeborn invited all of Red Wing to his home for a combination Thanksgiving and Christmas celebration that year. The occasion is remembered as the only time the entire white population of the town was assembled in one place.

William Freeborn's business and civic interests were far-reaching. In Red Wing he concentrated on real estate and was a partner in a sawmill, but he was also involved in enterprises in St. Paul, Albert Lea, and Cannon Falls. He served in the territorial legislature beginning in 1854, Freeborn County was named for him in 1855, and he was elected mayor of Red Wing in 1858. Freeborn also persuaded Hamline's founding fathers to locate the university in Red Wing in 1854. He was convinced that Red Wing would soon be "a center of money, population, and intelligence."

Partially funded by a gift of twenty-five thousand dollars in property from Bishop Leonidas Hamline of the Methodist Episcopal Church, Hamline was Minnesota's first private college. Its first principal, Reverend Jabez Brooks, opened a preparatory department for thirty-three students on the second floor of a downtown store on November 16, 1854. (A classicist, Brooks was later professor of Greek at the University of Minnesota.) The next year work was started on the school's two-story brick building on the plot of ground that is now Central Park. Bricks for the project were supplied by local brickyard owner George Wilkinson who also had the construction contract.

From the start the university was coeducational and students came not only from Minnesota, but also from Michigan, Iowa, and Wisconsin. The curriculum included four departments: Preparatory, Classical, Scientific, and Ladies' Graduating. Tuition was ten dollars a quarter (oftentimes paid in produce or by lodging the teachers); boarders paid two and a half dollars weekly. But making ends meet was always a problem. On at least one occasion the professors were reduced to dividing a single sack of flour among themselves. Supposedly, they carried it home by dead of night to keep towns-people from learning of their predicament.

One professor who came to Red Wing and stayed briefly at Hamline was Edward Eggleston. His novel, *The Hoosier Schoolmaster*, catapulted him to nationwide fame when it was published in 1871. Two years later another of his books, *The Mystery of Metropolisville*, portrayed the town of Red Wing as Red Owl. Financial problems forced Hamline to disband in Red Wing in 1869. When it reopened after reorganizing in 1880, it had moved to St. Paul.

A second early and illustrious visitor to Red Wing was Henry David Thoreau in June, 1861. Minnesota was being touted as a health resort at the time, and he was ailing with tuberculosis. (He died the next year at the age of forty-four.) Accompanied by a seventeen-year-old companion and protege, Horace Mann, Jr., Thoreau was traveling upriver when he decided to spend a few days in Red Wing. After signing in at the Metropolitan Hotel, the pair immediately hiked to the top of Barn Bluff to make their first observations. Mann wrote to his mother that he collected pasque flowers there for his Uncle Nat (Nathaniel Hawthorne, who was married to his mother's sister).

Thoreau opened and read his mail on Barn Bluff. "Too much could not be said for the grandeur and beauty" of the Mississippi River Valley in this region, he wrote. Making detailed lists of the local flora, he noted "pale spiked lobelia, bluer than common," "sow thistle, yellow flower," "wild cherry red," and "American rock cress" on Barn Bluff. Butterweed was prevalent "where the Indians had cultivated," and there was catchfly behind the hotel. He also mentions Red Wing's poisonous snakes: "Could have killed a hundred rattle-snakes a day six or seven years ago on Barn Bluff. Very thick on the hillside then. Three kinds in all. Yet nobody killed, though bitten. Yet made some sick sometime, a squaw last summer."

On one point, Thoreau was mistaken; Red Wing's snakes were lethal. Missionary Chauncey Hobart, describing his arrival in Red Wing in 1849, wrote in his memoirs: "Near the southwest corner of our present park, in a corn-field, stood a scaffold made of poles and bark. On top of this, and wrapped in a red blanket, with a white rag for a flag, fluttering at his head, lay an Indian. This man had died a few days before, in consequence of his ambition to be considered a 'Wau-kon,' or medicine man. In order to show that his claim to this honor was true, he had placed a rattlesnake in his blanket and carried it about, taking it out and handling it before the people and telling them on such occasions, 'You see the snake don't hurt me—I am "Wau-kon." ' But the snake had bitten him, and he, being too proud to acknowledge it and procure the necessary help, had received a fatal wound."

This photograph of the interior of Adolph Berg's restaurant and bakery on Main Street in Red Wing dates to the late 1800s.

Very quickly, because it was surrounded by fertile farmland, Red Wing became an important grain and marketing center. Wheat was the principal crop. John Day planted the first wheat grown in the county in Red Wing in 1853. The next year the firm of Hoyt and Smith built the first grain warehouse and started shipping wheat downriver. For almost two decades before the railroad era, farmers hauled their grain as far as fifty miles to Red Wing. This is also where the wheat futures market started. When the sleighing was good, farmers continued to bring their wheat to Red Wing during the winter. Grain buyers came up with the idea of financing this wheat by selling it for May delivery to a Chicago export house. These were the first sales of "May wheat."

By the late 1850s, with several hundred residents, Red Wing had eleven hotels, nine dry goods stores, two grocers, four clothing stores, three hardware dealers, a bookstore, three jewelry stores, two drug stores, two boot and shoe stores, a furniture store, and a fur store. Commercial buildings lined Main Street between Bush and Plum (then called Plumb), and other businesses were scattered along Bush and Plum streets as far north as Third Street. Red Wing's first newspaper, the *Red Wing Sentinel*, edited by William Colvill, was launched in 1855. A second and rival paper, the *Red Wing Republican*, with Lucius Hubbard at its helm, started publication in 1857. With good reason, they thought, optimistic citizens were predicting the town's population would reach twenty thousand by 1862.

Her Irish Godfather

Pretty Red Wing was flirting with prosperity, that much was obvious. Coaxed on by her girlish wiles, a twenty-three-year-old Irishman named James Lawther was among those settlers disembarking at her levee in 1855. He had come partly for his health. After emigrating from Ireland in his teens, he had lived with an uncle in Dubuque, where the city's scorching summers had undermined his frail constitution. His uncle had also entrusted him with a sizable sum of money to invest in Goodhue County farmland.

Remmler's Brewery was located on the northwest corner of Bush and Fifth streets. The business had been started by William Heising in 1861; after Heising died in 1873, his widow married Adolph Remmler who enlarged the brewery and made Remmler's beer the most popular brew in Red Wing.

Charles Johnston

Eva T. Lawther replaced the original wooden steps on the octagon house with concrete stairs extending in two directions to the walk in 1918.

Within a short time of his arrival in Red Wing, James Lawther was displaying an uncanny knack for making money. When the U.S. Land Office opened on the town's Main Street in 1855, Lawther set up a real estate office directly opposite. He also did business as a banker and a grain merchant. Eventually, his personal holdings included nineteen store buildings with apartments upstairs in downtown Red Wing, twenty homes within the city, and ninety farms in Goodhue County.

Incredibly enough, Lawther had been in town but two years and was still a bachelor when he built his flamboyant red brick octagon-shaped house in 1857. This was the same year that Red Wing was incorporated, and about the time that each of its leading citizens agreed to purchase a city block on which to build their homes. Surplus lots could be sold as the owners wished, and trees were planted to give Red Wing the look of a New England town. The Lawther house, on the block bounded by Hill, Third, Franklin, and Fourth streets, was the young port's most extraordinary residence.

Showy as it might be, the house was also built for practical reasons. According to architect Orson Squire Fowler, who built the first octagon house in Fishkill, New York, in 1847, the shape was both economical and efficient. This would have appealed to Lawther. Despite his prodigious wealth and his generous support for community projects, he counted pennies when it came to household expenses. An octagon, Fowler explained, enclosed one-fifth more space than a square of the same perimeter, thereby making it cheaper to build. A central spiral staircase eliminated the need for corridors; the cupola flooded the core of the house with light.

This kind of dwelling was also best-suited for healthful living, the architect maintained. Though his vitality was quickly restored after coming to Red Wing, James Lawther was always concerned with his physical well-being. (For days at a time he sometimes chose to remain in bed.) First and foremost, Fowler recommended an "elevated site" for the house. This guaranteed a fresh, dry atmosphere. "Nothing can be more unhealthy than for vegetables to decay in a deep cellar, where there is no chance for ventilation," he cautioned. "The effluvia and the poisonous gases, generated by the decomposed masses, ascend through the floor and corrupt the air which you and your children are to breathe, whereas, if your houses are sufficiently high, and windows arranged so that the open air can sweep through, you will save your doctor's bills."

But if Lawther was influenced by Fowler, he did not follow his advice to the letter. While Fowler favored gravel as the ideal construction material (for its economy and durability), Lawther built his house from locally-made brick. The cut stone for the foundation was probably imported from St. Paul. A spacious porch surrounded the entire house, and two flights of wooden stairs led to the lawn and street. Altogether, it was a grandiose house, exactly to Lawther's liking, and the only one of its kind in the village.

In 1859 the young tycoon married Evalyn Theresa Mann, from Michigan, who had come to Red Wing to visit her sister Sarah, the wife of pioneer lawyer William Phelps. (Phelps was register of the land office in Red Wing and later the town's mayor.) Eva T., as she was known, with her husband's fortune only increasing, remodeled the octagon house to its present shape in 1870. The added wing contained a first-floor kitchen which replaced the original kitchen in the basement, a large dining room, and ample servants' quarters. The spiral staircase was taken out, and the central chimney and fireplaces installed. Customarily, the house was filled with guests who sometimes stayed on for weeks at a time; Eva T. was praised as a charming and hard-working hostess.

Pretty Red Wing lived up to her promise and more for James Lawther. But the arrangement was never one-sided. In return for her favors, Lawther was godfather to the fledgling town for better than half a century. Active in Red Wing's civic and political affairs, he also saw to her social and cultural needs. Among other gifts, many of them anonymous, he donated land in the center of town for the Carnegie-Lawther Library, paid for an addition to the Presbyterian Church, and contributed more than fifty thousand dollars for a YMCA in 1910.

As an Irishman, however, a part of him hungered for his native soil. He and Eva T. made several visits there, and as he aged, these stays became longer and more frequent. About the turn of the century, he quit Red Wing altogether to live in Ireland. When he died and was buried there in 1916, the *Red Wing Republican* called his life "a blessing to the material and moral welfare" of Red Wing and Goodhue County. Afterwards, Eva T. returned to the cherished octagon house and lived there until her own death in 1932.

Red Wing's bicycle club in front of Christ Church. A bicycle path was built between Red Wing and Lake City in the 1890s, but farmers along the route protested the venture. Bicycles scared their horses and caused them to run away, they said. They retaliated by plowing up the bicycle path. This picture was taken before the present tower was added to the church in 1898.

The couple left no direct descendants. Their only son, James Louis, born in 1867, died in his early twenties of typhoid fever only four months after marrying Cora Dickinson White of Hudson, New York. Cora returned East following her husband's untimely demise, but in 1923 she came to live with Eva T. in Red Wing. Two years later Eva T. deeded the family home to her daughter-in-law for "one dollar, love and affection." After Cora's death in 1944, the house was sold and converted to a rest home. It was purchased by its present owners, Morris and Delores Callstrom, in 1973. The Callstroms have restored it to a private residence and sell antiques in a portion of the house.

Besides the octagon house, James Lawther was also responsible for a good part of Red Wing's rich legacy of Victorian architecture. Built in 1859, the Lawther Block at 202 Bush Street is the oldest of Lawther's commercial buildings. (Lawther's offices on the second floor of this building were maintained until 1958 when the Lawther estate sold its remaining Red Wing properties.) In 1864 Lawther put up the addition to this block at 204-208 Bush Street where the Koehler Book and Stationery Store is located. The building's present owner, Forrest Watson, has recently divided the second and third stories of this historic block into condominiums.

Across the street, Lawther built the business blocks at 207-209 and 211-213 Bush Street. There is also the Lawther Post Office Block at 301-303 Bush Street, the Lawther Park Block at 201-207 Plum Street, and the Lawther Block at 325-327 Main Street. All of these buildings went up prior to 1875. A decade later Lawther began construction of the Gladstone Block at 305-313 Bush Street in 1885. Built of native limestone, this is the most impressive local example of the Richardsonian Romanesque style of architecture.

In addition to these buildings that remain, much of what Lawther built is no longer standing. As early as 1857 a Lawther building on the corner of Main and Bush streets, the present site of the St. James Hotel, burned to the ground. Other Lawther structures have met with the wrecking ball. The Carnegie-Lawther Library, for instance, was razed in 1968 in favor of a new public library building. The original YMCA building has also been replaced. More recently, Lawther's Irish rowhouses, fronting John Rich Park, were demolished in 1981. Supposedly patterned after tenements in Ireland, these were built for blue-collar workers and their families. The property was purchased by the Erickson Diversified Corporation in the 1960s. While city and state preservationists waged a lengthy legal battle to save the buildings, the site is now a parking lot.

Shell racing was a favorite sport in Red Wing in the 1870s. The most talked-about contest took place in 1875 when Stillwater oarsmen challenged Red Wing's crew to a race. Stillwater supposedly had the advantage because one of its crew members, Norman Wright, was the champion single oarsman in the state. But three Red Wing conspirators, Hi Parks, E. L. Baker, and Frank Sterrett, pulled off an amazing coup.

In early June, a man named John B. Fox arrived in Red Wing and was hired as a clerk at Hi Park's grocery. Almost immediately he found his way to the waterfront where he informed the racing team that he was a pretty good oarsman himself. Put to the test, he proved so good, in fact, that he was invited to become a member of Red Wing's four-man crew.

On the day of the race in late June, the steamer *James Mean* brought hundreds of passengers from Stillwater and St. Paul to Red Wing. With nothing but the race on everyone's mind, the whole town was caught up in gambling fever; estimates of the amount of money that changed hands that day vary from twenty to seventy-five thousand dollars. The first race was between Norman Wright and John B. Fox, and Fox won handily. He was so far ahead of his opponent at one point that he stopped to splash water on himself and suck on a lemon. During the next race, the four-oared one that most of the money was on, things went from bad to worse for the Stillwater men. When it became apparent that they had lost the contest, they abandoned it without crossing the finish line and rowed glumly to the steamboat.

Red Wing might well have rested on her laurels, with no one being the wiser, except for a minstrel show that was in town that day. One of the troupers recognized John B. Fox as being none other than Ellis Ward, the world's best-known rower. That started a controversy between Stillwater and Red Wing, still unresolved, as to how ethical it had been to import Ward. It's a sure thing that Red Wing never gave up her winnings, however.

Speaking of Heroes

Pretty Red Wing takes an especial pride in her Civil War heroes. Immediately upon hearing that Confederate soldiers had captured Fort Sumter in April, 1861, Minnesota's Governor Alexander Ramsey pledged one thousand men to defend the Union. This was the first offer of troops from any state.

Days later at a rousing rally held in Red Wing's courthouse to organize a volunteer company, upwards of fifty men pledged "their lives, their fortunes and their sacred honor in upholding the stars and stripes against the rebellious assaults now made upon them." William Colvill was the first man to enlist in Red Wing and one of the first men to do so in the state. When the call came for volunteers that evening, both Colvill and Edward Welch raced over the backs of the chairs in an effort to head the line. Welch stumbled on the last seat as he reached for the pen, and in that split second Colvill seized it, saying: "You are next, Ed." Colvill was elected captain of the Goodhue County Volunteers (Company F of the First Minnesota Regiment). Welch was his lieutenant.

Three months later at Bull Run, Ed Welch, who had been a junior at Hamline when he was recruited, became Red Wing's first war hero. Though wounded in the hip, he refused aid and urged his men to stand fast against repeated Confederate assaults. When the Union lost that skirmish, Welch was left for dead on the battlefield. After being captured and held for several months in southern prisons, he was commissioned major of the Fourth Minnesota Regiment prior to his exchange.

The next year when the Dakota War erupted in his home state, Welch was recalled to Minnesota to fight under General Henry Sibley. At Wood Lake where the Indians made their last stand, he was wounded a second time. He died in Nashville in February, 1864, after returning to the South with the Fourth Minnesota. His body was returned to Red Wing for burial.

Lucius Hubbard, arriving in Red Wing in 1857, came to fame as a newspaperman, army officer, entrepreneur, and statesman. He was elected governor of Minnesota in 1881 and 1883.

William Colvill, also a veteran of Bull Run, earned his reputation at Gettysburg in 1863. In one of the most dramatic battles of the war, Colonel Colvill led the First Minnesota in a charge against overwhelming odds that left half their number, including Colvill, casualties. The former newspaperman is credited with helping stem the Confederate advance and changing the course of the war. In 1928 President Coolidge dedicated a memorial statue to Colvill in the Cannon Falls cemetery where he is buried beside his wife. In all the history of warfare, said Coolidge, "the charge at Gettysburg has few, if any equals and no superior." A similar bronze statue of Colvill was erected under the dome of Minnesota's state capitol.

Built in Cincinnati in 1854, the steamer *War Eagle* carried troops from Red Wing to St. Paul during the Civil War.

Lucius Hubbard, a twenty-one-year-old tinsmith with literary ambitions when he arrived in Red Wing from New York in 1857, likewise achieved greatness in the Civil War. Hubbard gave up the editorship of the *Red Wing Republican* to enlist in the Union army in December, 1861. Less than a year later, he was chosen colonel of the Fifth Minnesota Regiment. At Corinth, Mississippi, in October, 1862, he headed his troops in a hard-fought action that helped push the nearly-victorious southerners into retreat. Father John Ireland, the Fifth's chaplain (and later archbishop of St. Paul) described the feat ecstatically: "With what unanimity, with what rapidity, what visible coolness and unflinching courage, they poured volley after volley into the ranks of their opponents!"

Both Colvill and Hubbard, along with a third Red Wing man, Robert McLaren, attained the rank of brigadier general in the war. McLaren later served as commandant at Fort Snelling in the 1860s. Though crippled by war injuries, William Colvill practiced law in Red Wing where he lived to the age of seventy-five. Colvill Park on the town's waterfront is the site of his pioneer homestead. Lucius Hubbard became a wealthy merchant and railroad executive in Red Wing. In 1881 and again in 1883, he was elected governor of Minnesota.

With the Civil War behind her, Red Wing's prospects redoubled. The Homestead Act passed in 1862 was providing cheap land, and wheat prices were climbing. Once the river was open each spring, steamer after steamer landed a bevy of eager settlers at the port. Many of these came to farm on the surrounding prairie, but the town itself was attracting others.

Red Wing's present tannery is named for Silas B. Foot who was in the shoemaking business with G. K. Sterling in the 1860s on the corner of Main and Plum streets. The Ferrin Furniture Company is now on this site. Foot was the son of a Pennsylvania shoemaker and farmer, one of ten children, and had been selling patent rights to a pump when he came to Red Wing in 1857. In 1872, to keep pace with their leather needs, the two partners built Trout Brook Tannages, a three-story wooden tannery building with thirty vats in Featherstone Township.

These members of the Aurora Ski Club in 1890 are Paul Henningsted, Mikkel Hemmestvedt, Torger Hemmestvedt, and B. T. Hjermstad. The group sponsored ski jumping; it was organized in 1886 with C. H. Boxrud as its first president.

Benjamin and Daniel Densmore, brought to Red Wing by their parents in 1857, built the Red Wing Iron Works on Levee Street in 1866 to manufacture machinery and engines. (This is the city's oldest industrial building.) Other new businesses included Michael Kappel's wagon and carriage shop, a sorghum mill that produced sorghum sugar, William Heising's brewery, and a pork-packing plant. In 1867 the Cogel and Betcher factory, a company that made sash and doors and dated to 1856 in Red Wing, enlarged and improved its mill facilities. That same year Red Wing bowed to good times by erecting a three-story brick Music Hall on the corner of Main and Plum. (Now a parking lot, the site of the old Music Hall is marked by two pillars salvaged from the building when it was demolished in 1970.)

Briefly, there was an oil boom in Red Wing, started in 1866 by a resident who was digging for water. A stock company was formed to exploit the find, but the boom proved a bust when it turned out that a pair of pranksters were spiking the well by night with kerosene.

On a more serious note, two major fires in Red Wing in 1865 prompted the purchase that year of the town's first fire engines. After both the Howe, Daniels and Company sawmill and the Tee-Pee-Tonka Hotel burned to the ground in May and June, two hand engines and a pair of two-wheeled hose carts were purchased for slightly more than a thousand dollars from Springfield, Massachusetts. (Until then, wrote an early historian, Red Wing's firefighting apparatus consisted mainly of ten dozen wooden pails which "with praiseworthy beneficence, though with somewhat doubtful economy, the sages of the city had voted to insure [the town's property] against that dangerous element fire.") Equipment was not always the answer, though.

In 1869 the fire department splurged on a shiny new two-wheeled hose cart, the arrival of which prompted a grand ball on the top floor of the Music Hall. This was where the engine was when the Metropolitan Hotel caught fire. The problem was that the cart had been taken apart to get it up the two flights of stairs, then reassembled. To get it back down to the street, its wheels had to be removed. By the time it reached the scene of the fire, the hotel, valued at fifteen thousand dollars, had been destroyed.

Ninety-eight lives were lost in Red Wing's worst disaster when the steamer *Sea Wing* capsized near the middle of Lake Pepin on July 13, 1890. The crowded vessel was returning from a Sunday afternoon excursion downriver when it was struck by sixty-mile-an-hour winds. Nearly all of the victims were from Red Wing. They were privately interred, but a mass memorial service was held in the park on July 25. The obelisk bears the names of those who perished. Red Wing's undertaker, H. A. Allen, suffered a breakdown, incapacitating him for several months, as a result of the tragedy.

In 1870, amid considerable fanfare, the railroad arrived in Red Wing from
Hastings. Train service to St. Paul followed shortly. Going all out, Red Wing's
city council voted to spend $17.75 for champagne and $7.00 for wine to toast
the happy event. Tracks were also soon laid to Lake City and Winona. In 1871
Colonel Colvill become embroiled in a dispute with the railroad; he felt he
was being unfairly compensated for damage to his land near what is now
Colvill Park. The upshot was that he built a house on the railroad's grade,
covering a temporary track. When its workmen balked at challenging the war
hero, the railroad upped its award to him.

As the railroads reached deeper into the prairies, Red Wing's importance as a
wheat marketing center would decline. But for the time being the young town
was in her glory. In 1873 Red Wing was reportedly the largest primary wheat
market in the world. It had a warehouse capacity of one million bushels and
shipped nearly twice that amount of wheat and flour during the year. With
more than four thousand residents, Red Wing was also the state's fifth largest
city.

Red Wing's Goodhue
County National Bank
began as the Goodhue
County Savings Bank in
1874. T. B. Sheldon was
the first president. The
man on the far left is unidentified; the others are
Jesse McIntire, Fred
Busch, Jr., Freidrich
Busch, Sr. (the bank's
president from 1899 until
1906), and Sam Haynes.
The present bank build-
ing on the corner of Bush
and Third streets was
built in 1904.

This street fair in Red Wing in 1897 was photographed from the corner of Main and Bush streets. Barn Bluff is in the background.

The restored Bush Street entrance at the St. James Hotel.

Charles Johnston

The Unsinkable St. James

This kind of prosperity called for a new hotel. Built at a cost of sixty thousand dollars, the elegant St. James was underwritten by eleven prominent Red Wing businessmen: Joshua Pierce, Charles Betcher, William Brown, Jesse McIntire, E. L. Baker, Thor K. Simmons, John Friedrich, John Hack, Loren Smith, James Lawther, and Silas B. Foot. After two buildings on the site were razed in April, 1874, excavating began and the limestone foundation was finished in early July. G. A. Carlson, a local quarry owner, supplied both the limestone and thirty men for the job. Not so surprisingly, work had hardly commenced when an Indian grave was uncovered. Barely a foot underground, workers found two skeletons, a sardine box containing tobacco, and a hide scraper made from the leg bone of a deer.

By fall, the exterior brick walls were up and three storefronts on Main Street had been glassed in; crews plastered the inside walls during the winter. As soon as the first proprietors, E. J. Blood and F. A. Blood, signed a five-year lease, the interior decorators were called in. (It was common practice for proprietors to select the carpeting, drapes, and wallpapers.) The Blood brothers ordered expensive Brussels and English velvet carpets and "furniture of the finest manufacture to match," said a contemporary source. When the hotel opened to a lavish grand ball on Thanksgiving Day, 1875, nearly five hundred guests applauded pretty Red Wing's coming of age.

As might be expected, the fortunes of the St. James have paralleled those of the town. Begotten in boom times—champagne years—the hotel had every advantage while the bubbly lasted. The Blood brothers ran a first-class house and were highly praised for their efforts. A Minneapolis reporter rated the establishment "second to none in the state." According to local papers, the hotel was nothing less than a smashing success. Its guest rooms were usually filled and the dining room was equally popular. In 1877 the railroad changed its timetable to allow passengers time for a meal at the St. James.

But the good times were fleeting. The constant struggle to maintain a top-drawer hotel became too great for F. A. Blood. In 1878 he returned to Wisconsin where the brothers had been in the hotel business in Oshkosh. This left E. J. Blood to see to the St. James by himself until his death in 1885. After that, A. F. Graves, the local postmaster, stepped in to manage the property until 1890, when it closed for badly-needed repairs and remodeling. When it reopened in 1891, a new manager, Fred George, was at its helm. George remained with the hotel for five years to be followed by a succession of managers who came and went with amazing rapidity.

In 1905 Charles Lillyblad became the first manager to also own the hotel. Four years after it opened in 1875, Joshua Pierce and T. K. Simmons had bought out the hotel's other stockholders, making them the sole owners. Lillyblad struck a deal with Pierce for his shares in 1905. A few years later he purchased the remaining hotel shares from the Simmons family. The St. James stayed in the Lillyblad family for seventy-two years, and there were notable improvements.

Take, for instance, the well-appointed bar Lillyblad built next door to the hotel in 1917. This quickly went down the tube, however, when prohibition was voted into law the next year. More to the point was what the hotel owner did to the public baths. Marble went up on the walls and expensive tiling was laid on the floors. The fancy fixtures surpassed anything ever seen in Red Wing. Locals called it "Charley's Million Dollar Can." Farmers and laborers would come into town on Saturdays, buy a suit of underwear across the street at Johnson and Meyer, soak in a hot tub at Charley's, and toss their soiled garments in the hotel's garbage.

After Charley died in 1932, his wife, Clara, and their son, Art, ran the hotel for more than forty years. Clara was a hard-working woman, best-known for her cooking. In an article in the *Minneapolis Tribune* in 1959, George Grimm wrote that "for years travelers have stopped at Clara's place [where] the desk clerk will rent you a room with a magnificent view of the Mississippi for as little as $2.75 a night." Mentioning Clara's coffee shop, he added: "Red Wing folks know the food's always inviting." Art Lillyblad was born in the hotel, in room eighty-two in 1916, and grew up in it.

This is Main Street in the
1920s, looking towards
Barn Bluff. The St. James
is the four-story brick
building on the left.

Bobcats were so common in the area that there was open season on them year round in the 1890s. The hunter on the left is not identified; the others are Dr. Arnold Lees, Charles Crandall, and Bert Crandall. Dr. Lees was from England and came to Red Wing in 1890 when he was twenty years old. He was Red Wing's first veterinarian.

These members of Red Wing's volunteer fire department, photographed in 1876, are Henry Jenson, William Kuhn, and Karl Goebel. Their natty attire is typical for firemen of that era.

Butcher Ed Pirius posed for this Christmas portrait with his employees in front of his meat market at 226 Bush Street in 1888.

This ice palace was built
for the National Ski Tour-
nament held in Red Wing
in 1928.

In 1977, with the town's best interests in mind, the Red Wing Shoe Company purchased the hotel from Art Lillyblad (who stayed on as assistant manager). Downtown Red Wing needed a facelift and the restoration of the historic St. James was the keystone to its rejuvenation. Herb and Carol Bloomberg of Chanhassen (they own Chanhassen Dinner Theatres and the Chanhassen Furniture Galleries) were hired to do the remodeling and redecorating. Herb concentrated on remodeling and construction while Carol is the family's researcher and interior designer. So far the project carries a multi-million dollar price tag.

Nothing has been left undone. Every inch of the hotel has been redecorated, recarpeted, and refurnished. Its sixty guest rooms were reduced to forty-one to make some of them bigger and provide space for private baths in all of them. (Each of the bedrooms is decorated differently.) Downstairs in the formal 1870s lobby, the grand staircase, lined with portraits of the hotel's founding fathers, was moved to its original position facing Bush Street. There are three restaurants: the Victorian Dining Room (where Clara served her guests), the Port of Red Wing on the lower level, and a coffee shop. The hotel has also been enlarged; a new five-story addition that overlooks the river includes another nineteen guest rooms and party facilities.

The renewed St. James is a light-hearted version of the first hotel. For one thing, there was no way that Carol Bloomberg could duplicate the hotel's original furnishings. Not so much as a stick of furniture remains from those years. (Hotel managers customarily bought all their own furnishings and took everything with them, down to the last platter, when they moved to another position.) A search of period newspaper files didn't help much either. What descriptions there were of the hotel's rooms were scanty, Carol learned. The bridal suite, as an example, was reported to have been done in shades of rose "to reflect the rosy attitudes of its inhabitants."

Given the circumstances, Carol chose to underplay the Victorian. She didn't want it to get "sticky" or "overwhelming," she said. Preferring to let architectural detail show, she avoided heavy draping and re-draping of the windows. The furnishings she selected are an eclectic mix of antique and reproduction pieces that tend to reflect country styles. She also handpicked all of the pictures (some framed to let the wallpaper show through), photographs, and accessories for the rooms. Completing this nineteenth-century illusion, she ordered handmade pieced bed quilts for each of the guests rooms.

As fully expected, the ongoing rehabilitation of the hotel has triggered a revival of the downtown business district. Mirroring as it does the town's preoccupation with its past, the renewed St. James is a showpiece that bodes well for Red Wing's future.

From the Port of Red Wing

Chocolate Pecan Pie

Ingredients: One ten-inch unbaked pie shell
Chocolate chips
Chopped pecans
One quarter cup sugar
One quarter cup butter
One and one-half cups light corn syrup
Three eggs
One teaspoon vanilla

Cover bottom of pie crust scantily with chocolate chips. Spread enough chopped pecans over chips to cover generously. Beat eggs and set aside. Mix sugar, butter, and corn syrup together in a saucepan and bring to a boil for one minute. Pour mixture into beaten eggs while beating at high speed. Blend in vanilla. Pour into pie shell being careful not to disturb chocolate chips and pecans. Bake at 350° for forty-five minutes.

Pottery grave markers are common in and around Red Wing. Most of these are for children who died while their fathers were employed in the pottery industry. Louise Morley died of peritonitis and is buried at Oakwood Cemetery.

Potters and Potteries

Charles Johnston

Red Wing's world-famous pottery industry traces its beginnings to a German immigrant named Joseph Pohl. A potter by trade in his homeland, Pohl settled in Goodhue County in 1861, presumably to try farming. Quite by accident, it appears, his property turned out to be the future site of the area's clay pits. Using a homemade treadle-operated wheel, he fashioned bowls, jugs, and jars for neighboring housewives. He also made toy animals and whistles for their children. Two examples of his work—a coffee pot and a Turk's head baking pan—owned by the Goodhue County Historical Museum, attest to his proficiency. Pohl did not remain a potter, however. By 1874 he had moved to Featherstone township where his occupation is listed as "farmer." Just the same, Joseph Pohl had roused the sleeping giant.

In 1870 the *Goodhue County Republican* remarked on the "success which William Philleo seems to have attained in the manufacture of terra cotta at his grounds a short distance from the city." Philleo was producing a wide variety of earthenware crocks, jars, pickle jars, flower crocks, and hanging baskets at an establishment on Hay Creek Road, about two miles from downtown Red Wing. In addition to utilitarian pottery, the Philleo firm also made architectural trimmings. One such commission was for window caps and moldings for General Lucius Hubbard's elaborate red brick mansion in Red Wing. Some of the Hubbard terra cotta was ruined when the pottery went up in flames in July, 1870.

After rebuilding, the pottery called itself the Red Wing Terra Cotta Company and confined its output solely to architectural forms (window and door caps, cornices, and brackets) and statues and urns for gardens and cemeteries. One of the first jobs completed was the detail work for the Hubbard residence. This house stood at 1407 Fourth Street. It was purchased for use as St. John's Hospital in 1903; later, it was razed to make room for a new addition at the facility in the 1960s.

The Minnesota Stone-
ware Company, shown
here in 1893, was orga-
nized ten years earlier. It
burned to the ground in
1900 but was quickly
rebuilt.

The Philleo pottery also made the arched window caps for Philander Sprague's splendiferous new house at Third and Hill streets in 1874. Sprague was an early grain merchant and miller, and an associate with Philleo in the pottery business. Once described as a "Charles Addams version of what a Victorian mansion should be," the house is featured on the cover of Roger Kennedy's book, *Minnesota Houses*. Its present owner is Mrs. L. E. Claydon, the widow of Dr. L. E. Claydon who purchased it in 1903. Coincidentally, Dr. Claydon was also instrumental in founding St. John's Hospital that same year.

During the summer of 1981, when the city was excavating for a storm sewer, hundreds of pottery shards from the Philleo factory were uncovered by Red Wing resident and pottery collector Arlan Johnson who lives along Hay Creek Road. Working hurriedly around scheduled construction, Johnson found fragments of large architectural moldings similar to those on the Sprague house as well as scraps of utilitarian pottery and flowerpots. The site also yielded charred wooden beams and boards filled with old square nails. According to Johnson, this was possibly wreckage from the fire that destroyed the pottery in 1870. In 1880 William Philleo moved his company to St. Paul where it did business as Stillman and Philleo Terra Cotta Works until his death at the age of forty-five in 1885.

A second group of early Red Wing potters were former Philleo employees. On July 22, 1875, the *Red Wing Argus* reported that David Hallum, Henry Mitchell, and L. Bowman were making utilitarian stoneware in the backyard of Hallum's residence on the corner of Third and Minnesota streets. Hallum was a superb craftsman, but his firm didn't have a chance. Well-established potters in Akron, Ohio, had secured the market up and down the Mississippi, and they didn't welcome competition. From the look of things, this Red Wing upstart could usurp their entire northern trade. To prevent this from happening, they sold their wares at half price for as long as it took to drive him out of business.

Red Wing might have lost this first round when Hallum's enterprise collapsed, but local businessmen rallied to the challenge. The potential for a Red Wing pottery was obvious. C. C. Webster (of Webster's Way fame) organized the meeting on February 1, 1877, that led to the incorporation of the enormously successful Red Wing Stoneware Company only eight days later. Plans were laid for a large, forty by seventy foot building with the necessary adjacent structures, kilns, clay sheds, and a warehouse. In its first year of operation, the factory produced 270,000 gallons of stoneware and did better than forty thousand dollars worth of business on a capital investment of twenty-five thousand dollars.

Red clay sewer pipe was manufactured in Red Wing between 1890 and the 1970s.

As the town expanded its pottery market (it reached as far south as Missouri and included all of Minnesota, Dakota Territory, and northern Wisconsin), a second pottery set up in Red Wing in 1883. Many of those who invested in the new Minnesota Stoneware Company were also stockholders in Red Wing Stoneware. Pioneer businessman T. B. Sheldon, already in his sixties, was its president. (When he died at the age of eighty in 1900, Sheldon left half his estate, eighty-three thousand dollars, to the city of Red Wing. The money was used to build the T. B. Sheldon Memorial Auditorium—the first municipal playhouse in the United States.) A fire that began in a kiln shed consumed Red Wing Stoneware's works in 1884, but the older pottery was rebuilt and enlarged within months. By 1888 the Red Wing plants were said to be the largest stoneware establishments in the United States. Each factory had a work force of a hundred men, and between them, they consumed five thousand tons of clay annually.

Could it be that the town might do itself one better by adding still another pottery? Enough people thought so, and a third firm, the North Star Stoneware Company, was capitalized with one hundred thousand dollars in 1892. Its well-lighted three-story plant was more than two hundred feet long, and the engine house and clay shed stretched an additional hundred feet beyond that. Clearly, the facility was the envy of the two neighboring potteries. But it was also at a decided disadvantage.

The reason was timing. The Panic of 1893 idled all three potteries the next summer. This was a new experience for the two older firms. Neither of them had ever been shut down except in the days when clay was hauled to the potteries by horse cart and the roads became impassable in the spring. Work resumed at the three potteries in the fall, and they banded together to form a common sales agency, the Union Stoneware Company. But North Star wasn't improving its odds. It held only twenty-four percent of the Union's stock and according to agreed-upon terms, received a proportionate share of the orders. As a result, the North Star plant was unable to operate at or near its full capacity. The company folded and its factory stopped production when seven-eighths of its capital stock was purchased by owners of the other two potteries in 1896. The building later became part of the Red Wing Malting Company.

This building which housed the *Goodhue County News* at 211 Plum Street was finished with terra cotta moldings.

Clay for Red Wing's stoneware companies came from the clay pits in Goodhue township until 1928. Pictured with a clay loading car are Claus Fredine, Vernold Johnson (boy), Albin Johnson, and three unidentified persons.

Beginning in 1890 and continuing until the 1970s, Red Wing also used Goodhue County's native clay to make some of the world's best stoneware sewer pipe. The idea apparently originated with George Cook, an official at Red Wing Stoneware, at a time when the pottery was looking for ways to use surplus red clay. Vast heaps of the red-colored material had accumulated through the years because it invariably lay atop the deeper beds of fine gray clay. In a burst of ingenuity, Cook turned out a three-foot length of pipe and displayed it in the window of the Pierce Simmons bank with a sign asking: "Red Wing sewer pipe—why not?"

There were two competing companies at first, the Red Wing Sewer Pipe Company and the John H. Rich Sewer Pipe Company, until they merged in 1901 under the former name. In January, 1896, the *Red Wing Republican* reported on a contract contest for sewer pipe that Red Wing won handily. The Chicago suburb of Des Plaines had put out a bid for two-foot lengths of sewer pipe, twenty-four inches in diameter (standard was eighteen inches), with a crush resistance of 8,000 pounds. Put to the test, Red Wing sewer pipe withstood 28,340 pounds of pressure. The second-place product, from Monmouth, Illinois, fell to pieces at 9,980 pounds. By 1907 the Red Wing Sewer Pipe Company employed 250 workers.

Having weathered the economic turndown of the early 1890s, Red Wing's two surviving pottery factories were likewise in fine fettle by the turn of the century. Even though both plants burned to the ground within nine months of each other in 1900, they were rebuilt immediately. Pleased with the performance of their sales alliance, they also decided to combine their overall efforts. Red Wing Stoneware and Minnesota Stoneware officially reorganized in 1906 as the Red Wing Union Stoneware Company. From that time, Red Wing was left with a single pottery—but one that made its mark worldwide.

Prosperity continued in the next two decades while the pottery advertised all manner of jars (for pickles, salt pork, and sauerkraut), crocks, churns, and bowls. There were also flower pots and bean pots, water coolers and cuspidors, even chamber pots and bed warmers. In the late 1920s, when the market was bottoming out for some of these products, the company stayed in the black by introducing a new line of artware or finer vases. In the midst of the Depression, it began making dinnerware.

This is the office staff of the Northwestern Life Insurance Company in Red Wing about 1887. Seated in the middle is A. J. Meachum, the first president of the North Star Stoneware Company.

Red Wing dishes (made first in solid colors and later in dozens of hand-painted patterns) have since become collectors' pieces. The finer clay needed for their manufacture was imported from Tennessee, Kentucky, North Carolina, and Georgia. With the growing popularity of Red Wing tableware and a corresponding decline in the production of stoneware, stockholders voted to change the name of the Red Wing Union Stoneware Company to Red Wing Potteries in 1936. By 1947 the pottery had stopped making stoneware altogether and was a leader in the dinnerware field. The old Red Wing Stoneware building, a three-story frame structure that had been used for warehouse space in recent years, was taken down and replaced with a new factory salesroom.

The reasons for the demise of the pottery date to about 1950, when the impact of imported dishes began to be felt in the American marketplace. Although foreign-made dinnerware accounted for only ten percent of what was being shown in department stores that year, the ratio soon edged sharply upwards. By 1967, the year the pottery closed, imports were claiming ninety percent of this country's dinnerware sales.

Red Wing Potteries experienced its first year of loss in 1955. New management was brought in, but the deficits only increased. When Richard Gillmer (formerly a Red Wing sales representative in the Chicago area) was hired as president in 1958, the picture brightened. Due to general belt tightening and some product diversification, the pottery showed a consistent (if sometimes negligible) profit every year through 1966. In management's opinion, it still looked as if the pottery might have a future. These hopes came to a quick end when the pottery was shut down once and for all by a workers' strike that began June 1, 1967. Three months later, when the company was unable to meet union demands for higher wages, the ninety-year-old institution was liquidated.

The four-story brick potteries building (the former Minnesota Stoneware Company building dating to 1900) was subsequently purchased by John Nankivil of Winona. In October, 1981, Nankivil and Robert Durfey, also of Winona, announced plans to renovate the old factory. The remodeled complex has been dubbed The Pottery and houses retail shops and eateries, business and professional offices, and top-floor condominiums. Once a brooding ghost, The Pottery is a practical twentieth-century tribute to the clay giant who smiled both fame and fortune on Red Wing.

The Philander Sprague house, at 1008 West Third Street, with arched pottery window caps made by the Red Wing Terra Cotta Company.

A Talent for Genius

Dr. Charles N. Hewitt
with his youngest son,
Nat, at Christmastime,
1887. Nat died about two
years later.

Pretty Red Wing boasts an uncommon talent for nurturing genius. For starters, her celebrities include the scientist who invented Puffed Wheat and Puffed Rice, the first physician to produce and use smallpox vaccine in Minnesota, and the United States' first woman ambassador. It almost seems as if the community has a corner on star-making. In any case, she has been alloted more than her fair share of famous residents.

Frances Densmore, born in Red Wing in 1867, was one of the most remarkable women Minnesota has produced. The daughter of Benjamin Densmore (who, with his brother Daniel, started the Red Wing Iron Works a year earlier), Frances was a pioneer in the field of ethnomusicology. At a time when most of her generation of Americans were bent on eradicating Indian culture, Frances Densmore immersed herself in studying and preserving their music.

"I heard an Indian drum when I was very, very young," is how she explained her lifelong fascination. The Densmore home in Red Wing commanded a view of the Mississippi River. On an island opposite the town, there was a Dakota Indian camp. "At night, when they were dancing, we could hear the sound of the drum and see the flicker of their campfire," she remembered. "I fell asleep with my mind full of fancies about the interesting people across the Mississippi."

In 1884, when she was seventeen, Frances Densmore entered Oberlin Conservatory in Ohio to study piano, organ, and harmony. After graduating, she completed another two years of musical training in Boston before returning to Minnesota where she taught piano in St. Paul and Red Wing. In Minnesota, she also began a systematic study of American Indians. "For the next ten years," she wrote, "I soaked my receptive mind with what army officers wrote about Indians, and what historians wrote about Indians, along with some of the publications of the Bureau of American Ethnology....All this was preparation for my life work."

Frances Densmore is pictured here with a Blackfoot Indian, Mountain Chief. At her request, he is interpreting in sign language the song being played on the phonograph.

In 1905, accompanied by her sister Margaret, Frances made her first field trip to Ojibwe villages at Grand Marais and Grand Portage on Lake Superior. The next summer she collected songs from two Dakota women at Prairie Island. Shortly afterwards she convinced the Bureau of American Ethnology at the Smithsonian to begin funding her research. (She used her first grant of $150 to purchase an Edison recording machine.) During the next fifty years her work took her from the Pacific Northwest to the Florida Everglades. At the time of her death at the age of ninety in Red Wing in 1957, she had made more than three thousand recordings of Indian music and published more than twenty books and two hundred articles on the subject.

In 1867 a brilliant young physician, Dr. Charles N. Hewitt, settled in Red Wing. Hewitt had been trained at Albany Medical College in New York and had distinguished himself as a surgeon during the Civil War. From the beginning, his approach to medicine was a preventative one (he had stamped out typhoid epidemics among the troops by demanding the camps be made sanitary); later, he studied immunology with Louis Pasteur and others in Europe. In Red Wing, he pioneered the use of smallpox vaccine in Minnesota.

Carrying out his experiments in a barn-cum-laboratory on the outskirts of Red Wing, Hewitt produced the serum by infecting live calves with cowpox vaccine obtained from the Massachusetts State Board of Health. The animals' stomachs were shaved, then lined with row after of row of innoculations. When the innoculations festered, the vaccine was ready to use. During a smallpox scare in 1891, everyone in Red Wing was vaccinated.

On the first day of the mass innoculation, teachers marched their classes out to Hewitt's makeshift lab where an infected calf was tied bottom side up on a table. Mindful that many of the children were probably frightened, Hewitt demonstrated his technique on a fourteen-year-old volunteer, Maude Allyn. After gently scraping her arm with a knife, he rubbed the wound with some of the serum from one of the calf's sores. Within a few months, he had innoculated two thousand persons and is credited with averting a severe epidemic.

Lauris Norstad was the son of the pastor of St. Peter's Lutheran Church in Red Wing and graduated from Red Wing High School in 1925. Often referred to as the "boy wonder," he was the youngest officer to achieve the rank of Major General during World War II. In 1956 he was named Supreme Allied Commander in Europe of NATO. The Goodhue County Historical Museum in Red Wing owns a portrait of Norstad painted by Dwight Eisenhower. It also has Norstad's West Point uniform and his wife's inaugural gown.

Dr. Hewitt established Red Wing's first hospital, caring for indigent patients sent to him by the county in a house on West Third Street. He was also behind the bill passed by the legislature in 1872 that created the Minnesota State Board of Health. (For the next twenty years, he served as its executive secretary, operating out of the Keystone Building on Main Street in Red Wing.) Beyond this, he was elected president of the Minnesota State Medical Association in 1882 and president of the American Public Health Association in 1888. When Minnesota celebrated its centennial in 1958, Red Wing singled out Dr. Hewitt for special recognition in the Statehood Parade as the "father of public health."

Dr. Hewitt was married to the former Helen Robinson Hawley, the cousin of another pioneer Red Wing physician, Dr. A. B. Hawley. The Hewitt home, now replaced, was at Third and Hill streets. This is the corner that has been termed the most architecturally significant intersection in Minnesota. The octagonal Lawther house is across Third Street from the Hewitt site. The French Second Empire Sprague house is across Hill. Catercorner across both Third and Hill is the former E. S. Hoyt house, one of the finest examples of prairie school architecture in the Midwest. (E. S. Hoyt was president of the Red Wing Potteries and the Red Wing Sewer Pipe Company for several decades. Built in 1913, the house was designed by the firm of Purcell, Feick and Elmslie in the manner of Frank Lloyd Wright.)

In later years, Dr. Hewitt moved his farm laboratory to the frame building at 216 Dakota Street that now houses the Cloak Room clothing shop. (Owners Barb Delahunty and Ardee Rosasco chose the name after reading a description of the doctor "walking through Red Wing on his way to visit a patient at night with his cloak tossed over his shoulder and a lantern in his hand.") Unusual in Red Wing because of its Colonial saltbox architecture, the building has recently been stripped of its "Depression brick" asphalt siding to reveal the original clapboard. It has also been placed on the National Register of Historic Places.

Dr. Alexander P. Anderson of Red Wing invented Puffed Wheat and Puffed Rice.

A. P. Anderson Park in west Red Wing is named for Dr. Alexander P. Anderson who invented Puffed Wheat and Puffed Rice. Anderson was born in nearby Featherstone township in 1862, the sixth of seven children of Swedish immigrant parents. Until he was eighteen, he attended the local one-room school and worked on the family farm. After that, having passed the state examinations, he taught in the same school to earn the money to go to college. He attended the University of Minnesota for a year, but his funds ran out and his father needed him on the farm. Returning home, he divided his time between teaching in nearby country schools and working in the fields for the next several years.

Following the deaths of his parents, Anderson went back to the university in 1890, paying his way by carrying papers, shoveling snow, and tending furnaces. With the help of a scholarship, he had six hundred dollars in the bank when he was awarded a Master of Science degree in 1895. With this as seed money, he borrowed the balance to take him to Munich for a year where he received his doctorate. In Munich, he also became intrigued with the Meyer starch granule theory. When he came back to this country, it was with the hope of being able to do research in this area. In the meantime, he taught botany at Clemson College in South Carolina. In 1898 he married Lydia McDougall Johnson from Glasgow, Scotland, at Highlands, North Carolina.

In 1901, when Dr. Anderson accepted a position as curator of the Herbarium at Columbia University in New York, he did so because it meant that he would would be allowed to pursue his research at the New York Botanical Garden. That same year, while studying the nature of starch granules, he discovered the process of puffing cereal grains. Rice, wheat, barley, buckwheat, and other grains were heated to high temperatures in glass tubes which were then broken, causing the cereal grains to explode. Realizing the commercial possibilities of puffed grains, Dr. Anderson obtained patents on his procedures and entered into an agreement with the Quaker Oats Company to produce and market the cereals. At first, puffed grains were considered a confection; bags of puffed rice were sold like popcorn at the World's Fair in St. Louis in 1904.

Enoch (Nickie) Johnson's garage on Plum Street was the first one in Red Wing to repair automobiles. Johnson is the man on the left. A skilled and inventive mechanic, he built Red Wing's most unusual car, a flashy eight-wheeled open model, from the parts of wrecked Dodges. (It was later acquired by a museum in Elkton, South Dakota.) Johnson also played the violin and headed an eight-piece band that played in and around Red Wing for many years.

For the next thirty-five years, Dr. Anderson conducted more than fifteen thousand experiments for Quaker Oats. He also designed the complicated machinery needed to manufacture the cereals. Initially, he worked at the company's laboratories in Chicago, but in 1915 he returned to Red Wing to start building Tower View. Located at the present intersection of highways 61 and 19, the complex consisted of a family home, farm buildings, a water tower, ice house, greenhouse, and two laboratory buildings where Dr. Anderson conducted his research. Built to last several lifetimes, the buildings were constructed of reinforced concrete with red brick facing and red tile roofs. A matching brick wall fronted the estate; the property encompassed approximately one thousand acres.

Two of Dr. Anderson's daughters, Elizabeth and Jean, and his only son, John, still live in Red Wing. Elizabeth Anderson Hedin is the widow of Dr. Raymond Hedin whose partnership practice with Dr. Edward Juers in 1932 led to the establishment of the Interstate Clinic. Dr. Hedin also served two terms as Red Wing's mayor in the 1940s. In 1975 Elizabeth Hedin was the first woman to receive the C. C. Ludwig Award for outstanding municipal service from the League of Minnesota Municipalities.

Jean Anderson Chesley has been the president of the Goodhue County Historical Society for many years and is married to Dr. Frank Chesley. Together with Dr. Demetrius Jelatis and Dr. Gordon Lee, former classmates of his at the Massachusetts Institute of Technology, Dr. Chesley founded Central Research Laboratories at Tower View in 1945. Currently the world leader in the development and production of master-slave devices, the company occupied Dr. Anderson's former laboratories until 1961. Since that time the firm has had its own building across Highway 61 from Tower View. In 1979 Central Research Laboratories was acquired by Sargent Industries which, in turn, was bought by the Dover Corporation in 1984. In 1975 the Anderson family donated Tower View, including 343 acres, to The Nature Conservancy. The land and buildings were subsequently conveyed to the Red Wing school district; the property is now the Red Wing Energy Education Center.

John Anderson, Dr. Anderson's son, is an artist and photographer. His wife, Eugenie Moore Anderson, became the United States' first woman ambassador when she was appointed to Denmark by President Truman in 1949. Stopping briefly in Red Wing in 1952, Truman called Eugenie Anderson "the finest human being I know." In 1962 she was named minister to Bulgaria by President Kennedy. Since 1932 John and Eugenie Anderson have lived on the east side of the Anderson property adjacent to Tower View.

The Roland Conklin family has expertly restored this classic Victorian residence at 1022 East Avenue.

Red Wing also has a world-class artist in Charles Biederman who moved to Red Wing in 1942. Misunderstood by some and unappreciated by others, Biederman's New Art is nonetheless a major innovation in American art. His brightly-colored metal reliefs have been exhibited at the Stedelijk Museum in Amsterdam, the Kunstgerwerbemuseum in Zurich, and the Galleria Milano in Milan. Museums in New York, Atlanta, Pittsburgh, Denver, Chicago, Dallas, Austin, and Akron have also shown his work. Major one-man exhibitions have been sponsored by the Walker Art Center in Minneapolis in 1965, the Hayward Gallery of London in 1969, Dayton's Gallery 12 in Minneapolis in 1971, and the Minneapolis Institute of Arts in 1976-77 (at 250 pieces, the largest exhibition by a Minnesota artist held at the Institute).

Charles Biederman was born in Cleveland in 1906, the son of Czech immigrants who came to America at the turn of the century. His father had been a blacksmith and eventually found work as a foreman in a storage house. When young Biederman entered school, he knew only Czech. He grew up thinking of himself as an outsider and still considers himself one. "If you are going to be a genuine artist, you have to buck the mob," he believes. Biederman is a controversial artist who has done just that.

Before World War II when he stated that the New Art would be machine art—that canvas and brush could no longer be viable media for contemporary artists in a technological age, he was ostracized by the art community in this country and abroad. "I was something you didn't talk about after that," says Biederman. He acknowledges only two artists as his direct predecessors: French Impressionist Claude Monet (1840-1926) and Postimpressionist Paul Cezanne (1839-1906). What he has done, he says, is carry forward and develop the discoveries made by these two artists. He would like to see his three-dimensional art reproduced in unlimited editions and available to everyone—much like phonograph records.

By the time he was sixteen, Biederman was working as an apprentice in a commercial art studio and saving his money to go to art school. He enrolled at the Art Institute in Chicago in 1926, but soon clashed with his teachers over what he called the antiquated artistic ethos and study program at the school. Though he was considered a gifted student and received scholarships for his second and third years, he left the school without graduating.

Charles Johnston

Fellow artist and friend John Anderson of Red Wing was Biederman's first patron. Anderson's support helped Biederman establish a studio in New York in the 1930s; it also enabled him to spend time in Paris where he met many artists including Picasso. In 1941 Biederman married Eugenie Anderson's sister, Mary Katherine Moore. Mary taught second grade in Red Wing, and Biederman was able to pursue his art in John Anderson's shop. He was nearly fifty before he had his own studio in Minnesota, located on a secluded piece of property that Mary found about a mile from the Andersons.

Unveiled in 1969, one of Biederman's complex abstract structures is on permanent display in Jordan Court in Red Wing. It was paid for in part by a substantial grant from the National Endowment for the Arts. Biederman has also published four provocative books: *Art as the Evolution of Visual Knowledge*, 1948; *Letters on the New Art*, 1951; *The New Cezanne*, 1958; and *Search for New Arts*, 1979. According to the artist, the latest book is his best and last. As he has always done, Biederman continues a rigorous work schedule, seven days a week. "I never stop. I never stop," he says. "If I did, it would be the end of me. The supreme quality of human life is to be creative."

The Best Is Yet To Come

With her heyday as a wheat queen behind her, pretty Red Wing is no less secure in her future. This is not a pushy town. She's never had a boom or a bust, but her underpinnings are secure. Diversified industry, both now and in the past, has insured her economic stability.

In this century, the shoe industry has become the backbone of the community. The Red Wing Shoe Company is the city's largest employer with more than nine hundred workers in its two Red Wing plants. Founded in 1905, the locally-owned firm produces industrial work shoes and boots and Irish

The T. B. Sheldon home, built in 1876 at Fourth and Fulton streets, is on the National Register of Historic Places. Frances Densmore lived here for several years in the 1950s after it had been divided into apartments.

78

Setter sports boots. Using a good share of the leather processed by the nearby
S. B. Foot Tanning Company, it turns out eight thousand pairs of boots daily,
fifty weeks a year. Also in the shoemaking business, a former Red Wing Shoe
employee, Paul Riedell, put together his own company to make boots for ice,
hockey, and roller skates in 1945. Riedell Shoes now employs 135 workers at a
factory across the street from Red Wing Shoe in the industrial park.

Other Red Wing industries include ITT Meyer Industries, with more than two
hundred employees, which produces tapered steel power transmission poles
for utility companies throughout the United States. This company began as a
three-man machine shop in Red Wing in 1930. It was purchased by ITT for
forty-four million dollars in 1972. Red Wing's milling industry is also still a
viable one. The Red Wing Mill, operated by the Archer Daniels Midland
Company, processes wheat flour, flax, and soybean meal and oil. Barley is
processed at Fleischmann Malting and Red Wing Malt. Another manufacturer,
Josten's Red Wing plant, is the world's largest producer of high school and
college diplomas; customers include Columbia University, Duke University,
Dartmouth College, and Stanford University.

Content in her middle-age, Red Wing is hardly suffering growing pains. Her
population, something less than fourteen thousand, is little more than it was
a decade ago. Unlike certain of her neighbors, she has no inclination to
become a bedroom community for the Twin Cities. At the same time, the
geographic size of the city increased dramatically in 1971 when Red Wing and
Burnside Township were consolidated. When this happened, placing the
Northern States Power nuclear plant on Prairie Island on Red Wing's tax rolls,
the city overnight became the most affluent municipality in the state.

As a result, with the exception of Minneapolis, Red Wing spends more money
per capita on services than any other city in Minnesota. It has twenty-three
full-time policemen, twenty-seven full-time firemen, and garbage is picked up
twice a week. (All of Red Wing's garbage, incidentally, is burned at a city-
owned facility on Bench Street which supplies steam heat for the tannery next
door.) By the same token, real estate taxes are a fraction of those paid by
homeowners with comparable property elsewhere in the state.

This balloon was
launched on the corner of
Fourth and Bush streets
in 1895.

Red Wing's *Number 7*, a
California transplant,
pulls up in front of The
Pottery.

Charles Johnston

Tom Lutz, a well-known figure in Minnesota preservation circles, calls Red Wing "an old-fashioned town that's coming back into fashion." Its retail stores are still concentrated in the downtown area, mostly in business blocks from the last century. Its central residential neighborhoods are still intact. Physically, the town has been spared any major deterioration. "Every corner of the town has got some qood quality to it," says Lutz, "whether it's blue collar quality or high art Victorian quality."

The concern now is to preserve Red Wing's nineteenth-century river town image. Former Mayor Ed Powderly (who died in office in 1984) saw this as his particular mission, focusing his attention on Red Wing's downtown commercial district. "Every city has got to have character in its downtown core," he explained. "As that core disappears and moves to the suburbs, some of the city's character is destroyed." Since 1976 Red Wing has also had a seven-member Heritage Preservation Commission, committed to identifying, preserving, restoring, and maintaining Red Wing's historic resources.

To date, three local historic districts, the St. James Hotel Historic District, the Heritage Mall District, and the newly-created Downtown Historic District, have been approved by the city council. The largest of these is the downtown district which includes eighty-five buildings, sixty of which were built before 1900. In addition, more than twenty individual buildings, structures, and sites as well as two districts, the Historic Mall District and the Red Wing Residential Historic District, have been placed on the National Register. Considering Red Wing's size, this record is nothing short of astounding.

Once the Red Wing Shoe Company had involved itself in reviving the St. James, private citizens undertook their own commercial restoration projects. The Richard Tittle family, for example, concentrated on turn-of-the century photographer Ed Lidberg's former studio at 312 West Avenue. Originally, the building had occupied the site of the Auditorium Theatre and was moved to its present location on rollers by horses in 1902. When the Tittles were finished with it, their firm and three others moved into the four-office complex.

More recently, Richard and Barbara Tittle, together with Samuel and Barbara Blue, have formed the 2B Corporation to restore a frame office building once occupied by the Red Wing Stoneware Company and the John H. Rich Sewer Pipe Works. Dating to the 1870s, the structure had been moved from its early site and converted to a one-family home. After it was condemned because it stood in the way of a road project, the Tittles and the Blues bought it for one dollar and moved it to 2233 Old West Main. The renewed building has been enlarged and will house office and retail space.

On Main Street, it would be hard not to notice what Don and Joleen Jensen, owners of Jensen Jewelers, have done for the Keystone Building. With its heavily rusticated ornamental brickwork, the Keystone Building is the finest remaining example of Italianate commercial architecture in downtown Red Wing. Daniel C. Hill (who also helped organize the Red Wing Stoneware Company) built the Keystone Building in 1867, and it first housed the J. C. Pierce and Thor K. Simmons Bank for fourteen years. Later, Dr. Hewitt had an office in the building. Many ideas for the restoration came from seeing a similar project in Salt Lake City, said Don Jensen. Whether or not his business would improve as a result of the work was never uppermost in his mind. "Red Wing is my home," he said. "I believe in investing in downtown Red Wing."

The earliest brick commercial buildings in downtown Red Wing had plain brick walls, rectangular or slightly arched windows, and wooden storefronts. The only remaining, relatively unaltered examples of this utilitarian style of architecture (Mid-Nineteenth-Century Commercial) are the Lawther Block at 202 Bush Street, built in 1859, and the addition which was added to it at 204-208 Bush Street in 1864.

During the 1860s more elaborate Round-Arched Romanesque commercial buildings were popular in Red Wing, to be followed by Italianate, Late Nineteenth-Century Commercial, Richardsonian Romanesque, Classical Revival, and Early Twentieth-Century Commercial structures. Copying patterns that had originated in the East, most of these buildings were designed and built by a small body of Red Wing architects who also doubled as contractors. Some of these men had more than local reputations.

Charles Johnston

Margaret Betcher built the Betcher Memorial Chapel at Oakwood Cemetery in memory of her husband, Charles Betcher, in 1906. Betcher was born in Prussia in 1830 and came to Red Wing where he became a leading businessman in 1856. The entrance gate, constructed of identical stone to complement the chapel, was the gift of E. H. Blodgett in memory of his wife in 1907.

Daniel C. Hill was the general contractor for the first Goodhue County Court-house and may have been responsible for a number of other buildings in downtown Red Wing that mimic its Romanesque styling. These include the Clark & Hawley, Lawther, and T. F. Towne Blocks, 321-329 Main Street, and Wallower's Block, 212-214 Bush Street. Hill also designed the S. D. Greenwood Block at 302 Plum Street, the Congregational churches in Zumbrota and Mazeppa, and several buildings including the town hall in Northfield. In Wisconsin, he drew the plans for the Pierce County Courthouse in Ellsworth, and a hotel and block of stores in Hudson.

By the turn of the century, William J. Loncor was Red Wing's premier builder. In addition to the Post Office, he built the Goodhue County Co-operative Store at 420-430 Third Street, the Busch Garage at 425-429 Main Street, and the I.O.O.F. Hall at 313-317 Third Street. A Minneapolis architect, Lowell C. Lamoreaux, also left his mark on downtown Red Wing. Lamoreaux's preference for Neoclassical designs (which gained favor after the Chicago Exposition in 1893) is reflected in the T. B. Sheldon Auditorium, the Goodhue County National Bank Building, and the Red Wing City Hall.

Besides these men, there was also Ambrose Clum, a self-styled architect and peculiar sort of man who first advertised his services in Red Wing in 1871. After building the Italianate Clum Block at 309-313 Plum Street in 1873, he designed the similarly-styled Hotel de Batlo at 325-327 Plum Street and the Union Block at 410-412 Third Street. He also designed St. John's German Lutheran Church at the corner of East Avenue and Fifth Street and supervised the construction of the La Grange Mill in 1877. By then, he had apparently had his fill of architecture.

During the next ten years, Ambrose Clum marketed a patent medicine (Dr. Clum's Liver Cathartic), founded a short-lived horse life insurance company, earned an M.D. from the Eclectic College of Physicians, was admitted to the Minnesota State Bar, and ran for the state senate. In 1890 he returned briefly to his earlier calling, designing the county poor farm house in Burnside, the First State Bank of Zumbrota, and the Pine Island Opera House. But in 1894, chucking it all, he moved to Minneapolis where he quickly established himself as a German tumor specialist.

A game of Chinese checkers, perhaps? The library at the St. James invites guests to relax in Victorian ambience.

Charles Johnston

If anything, the excitement generated by the preservation movement in Red Wing is only on the upswing. In the older residential neighborhoods, increasing numbers of homeowners are putting time and money into restoring their properties. With the downtown designated a historic district, property owners in the area are proving more eager to invest in their buildings. On Plum Street, the Armory and Masonic Hall has been remodeled for use as a restaurant with commercial and office space. Both the Clum Block and the Clark & Hawley Block at 329 Main Street also have newly improved apartments on their upper floors. (The Clark & Hawley Block was built in 1866 by A. J. Clark and Dr. A. B. Hawley to house their wholesale retail drug store.)

The long and short of it is that the city's surest bet for the future lies in remembering and building on her colorful past. Designation of the downtown as a historic district has made this easier to do. First of all, the area is protected against adverse changes within it; applications for building permits are reviewed by the Heritage Preservation Commission. New construction in the area needs to complement its historic nature, and changes or alterations to existing buildings must be in keeping with the structure's original design. (All buildings are considered to be products of their own time, however, and alterations that seek to create an earlier appearance are discouraged.) Secondly, because of recent tax law changes, property owners in the district are eligible for substantial tax credits for preserving and reusing historic buildings.

Victorian dress becomes pretty Red Wing. Her identity relies on her girlhood image. One of the last wooden riverboats, the *Pretty Red Wing*, plies the city's harbor, catering to sightseers. On Highway 61, a Hardee's hamburger restaurant does business in the former Chicago Great Western Depot. Red Wing's *Number 7*, a recently-acquired turn-of-the-century California cable car, is also operating between the St. James and The Pottery. Indeed, given her present frame of mind, pretty Red Wing's future is well-nigh assured.

If she ever had any doubt about it, the best is yet to come.

Selected Bibliography

Angell, Madeline. *Red Wing, Minnesota, Saga of a River Town.* Second edition. Minneapolis: Dillon Press, 1978.

Angell, Madeline, and Miller, Mary Cavaness. *Joseph Woods Hancock, The Life and Times of a Minnesota Pioneer.* Minneapolis: Dillon Press, 1980.

Bendix, Deanna Marohn. "There Is No Other Reason For Living." *Twin Cities* 5:2 (February, 1982).

Blegen, Theodore C. *Minnesota, A History of the State.* Minneapolis: University of Minnesota Press, 1963.

Carley, Kenneth. *Minnesota in the Civil War.* Minneapolis: Ross & Haines, 1961.

————. *The Sioux Uprising of 1862.* St. Paul: Minnesota Historical Society, 1976.

Curtiss-Wedge, Franklyn. *History of Goodhue County.* Chicago: H. C. Cooper, Jr., & Co., 1909.

Folwell, William Watts. *A History of Minnesota,* Volume II. St. Paul: Minnesota Historical Society, 1924.

Gebhard, David, and Martinson, Tom. *A Guide to the Architecture of Minnesota.* Third printing, corrected. Minneapolis: University of Minnesota Press, 1980.

Gillmer, Richard S. *Death of a Business: The Red Wing Potteries.* Minneapolis: Ross & Haines, 1968.

Gilman, Carolyn. *Where Two Worlds Meet.* St. Paul: Minnesota Historical Society, 1982.

Hancock, J. W. *History of Goodhue County, Minnesota.* Red Wing: Red Wing Printing Co., 1893.

Hobart, Chauncey. *Recollections of My Life. Fifty Years of Itinerancy in the Northwest.* Red Wing: Red Wing Printing Co., 1885.

Holst, Gladys. *The Octagon House.* Red Wing: Published by the author, 1974.

Hughes, Thomas. *Indian Chiefs of Southern Minnesota.* Reprint edition. Minneapolis: Ross & Haines, 1969.

Johnston, Patricia Condon. "The Moon Shines on Pretty Red Wing." *Twin Cities* 4:6 (June, 1981).

Kennedy, Roger. *Minnesota Houses, An Architectural & Historical View.* Minneapolis: Dillon Press, 1967.

Meyer, Roy W. *History of the Santee Sioux.* Lincoln: University of Nebraska Press, 1967.

————. "The Prairie Island Community, A Remnant of Minnesota Sioux." *Minnesota History* 37:7 (Fall, 1961).

Pike, Zebulon M. *The Expeditions of Zebulon Montgomery Pike.* Ed. by Elliott Coues. Reprint edition. Minneapolis: Ross & Haines, 1965.

Rasmussen, C. A. *A History of the City of Red Wing, Minnesota.* Red Wing: Published by the author, 1933.

Red Wing Daily Republican Eagle. *Goodhue County's First Hundred Years.* Red Wing: Goodhue County Historical Society, 1954.

Tefft, Gary and Bonnie. *Red Wing Potters & Their Wares.* Menomonee Falls, Wisconsin: Locust Enterprises, 1981.

Ullmann, Mrs. Joseph. "Frontier Business Trip." *Minnesota History* 34:1 (Spring, 1954).

Viel, Lyndon C. *The Clay Giants.* Des Moines: Wallace-Homestead Book Co. 1977.

Viel, Lyndon C. *The Clay Giants, Book 2.* Des Moines: Wallace-Homestead Book Co., 1980.

Besides these sources, Carrie Conklin's *Downtown Red Wing Historic Resources Inventory,* a study prepared for the city in 1983, proved very helpful. I also used the newspaper files at the Red Wing Public Library as well as research material contained in the files of the Goodhue County Historical Museum. Information concerning the St. James was supplied by the hotel, much of it in a booklet titled *The St. James Hotel— A history with a future,* published by the Red Wing Hotel Corporation in 1979. In addition, numerous Red Wing residents provided information about themselves, their families, and their businesses.

Index